GODDESSES

from A to Z

Copyright © 2019 by Ellen Lorenzi-Prince

Library of Congress Control Number: 2019936090

Designed by Brenda McCallum

Type set in Algerian/ITC Officiana

ISBN: 978-0-7643-5796-1
Printed in China

Published by Red Feather Mind, Body, Spirit
An imprint of Schiffer Publishing, Ltd.
4880 Lower Valley Road
Atglen, PA 19310
Phone: (610) 593-1777; Fax: (610) 593-2002
E-mail: Info@schifferbooks.com
Web: www.redfeathermbs.com

For our complete selection of fine books on this and related subjects, please visit our website at www.schifferbooks.com. You may also write for a free catalog.

Schiffer Publishing's titles are available at special discounts for bulk purchases for sales promotions or premiums. Special editions, including personalized covers, corporate imprints, and excerpts, can be created in large quantities for special needs. For more information, contact the publisher.

We are always looking for people to write books on new and related subjects. If you have an idea for a book, please contact us at proposals@schifferbooks.com.

Other Schiffer Books on Related Subjects:

Rupert's Tales: Making More Magick, Kyrja, illustrated by Tonia Bennington Osborn, ISBN 978-0-7643-5124-2

Rupert's Tales: The Wheel of the Year Beltane, Litha, Lammas, and Mabon, Kyrja, illustrated by Tonia Bennington Osborn, ISBN 978-0-7643-3689-8

Rupert's Tales: The Wheel of the Year Activity Book, Kyrja, illustrations by Tonia Bennington Osborn, ISBN 978-0-7643-4020-8

ELLEN LORENZI-PRINCE

GODDESSES *from*

A
TO
Z

REDFeather™
MIND | BODY | SPIRIT

4880 Lower Valley Road, Atglen, PA 19310

CLOSER THAN MY SKIN
GODDESS, YOU'RE WITHIN!

WITHIN A BOY, WITHIN A GIRL
WITHIN THE TREES, WITHIN THE WORLD.

Who Are the Goddesses?

Goddesses are beings of great power, beauty, and mystery. A goddess can be a woman from the spirit world, or she can be a force of nature wearing the face of a woman. Goddesses have been part of our history for thousands of years, and they guide and inspire people today.

Included in this ABC book are goddesses from all around the world, from Australia to Asia, Africa, Europe, and the Americas. The map on the next pages shows where each of these goddesses began.

There are many goddesses, but here are 26 of them—a goddess for each letter of the alphabet!

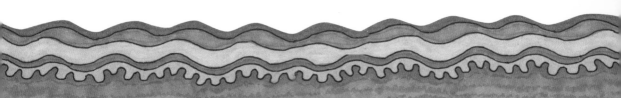

KEY

This map highlights the countries of origin of the ABC goddesses.

GODDESS	COUNTRY
A Artemis	Greece
B Brigid	Ireland
C Crow Mother	US (Arizona)
D Durga	India
E Epona	England
F Fortuna	Italy
G Gaia	Greece
H Haya-Akitsu-Hime	Japan
I Isis	Egypt
J Julunggul	Arnhem Land
K Kwan Yin	China
L Lady of the Lake	England
M Maat	Egypt
N The Norns	Norway
O Oya	Nigeria
P Pele	US (Hawaii)
Q Mama Quilla	Peru
R Rhea	Greece
S Samovila	Bulgaria
T Tara	Tibet
U Ushas	India
V Vesta	Italy
W White Buffalo Calf Woman	US (South Dakota)
X Xochiquetzal	Mexico
Y Yemaya	Nigeria
Z The Zorya	Russia

NORTH AMERICA

W

C

X

P

SOUTH AMERICA

Q

A IS FOR ARTEMIS
Artemis *(AR-tim-iss)* is from Greece.

She is the goddess of wild animals and the wilderness where the animals live. She is never afraid of ferocious animals because she knows she is stronger. Artemis runs through the forest with her friends and dogs during the day, and dances beneath the trees with them at night.

This goddess is strong, but always gentle with newborns, whether they are fawns or cubs or babies. She helps the mothers and protects their little ones. Artemis guards all that is innocent and pure, including the forest springs and streams of clear water.

Artemis will never live in a house or a town. She stays free to run through the woods as she likes with companions who want to be as free as the animals—as free and strong as she is.

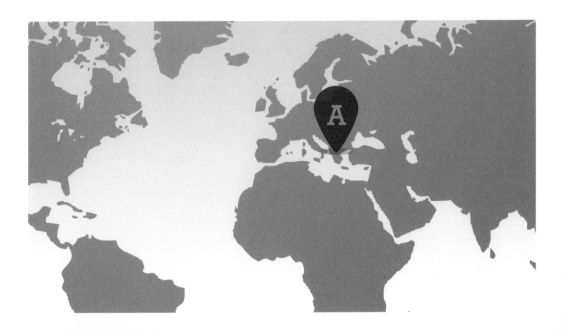

B IS FOR BRIGID
Brigid (*BRIJ-id*) is from Ireland.

Her name means Bright Arrow. She is a light that can touch you from afar, like a sunbeam or a smile or a great idea.

Brigid is a goddess of both fire and water. She is the goddess of what happens when two opposites work together: the energy of fire and the wisdom of water. Brigid is the goddess of smithcraft, poetry, and healing.

Smithcraft is making tools out of metal, like a knife you can use to cut your food. Irish poetry includes songs and stories of the people's history and the adventures of the gods and goddesses. Healing is what helps people feel better when they are sick or hurt. As the goddess of healing, Brigid knows how to use plants to make good medicine. She cares for her people by teaching and inspiring them to create the things that help make the world better.

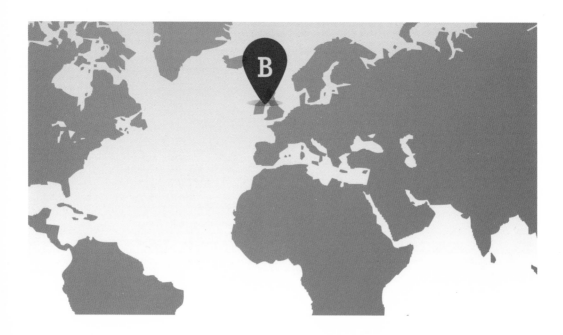

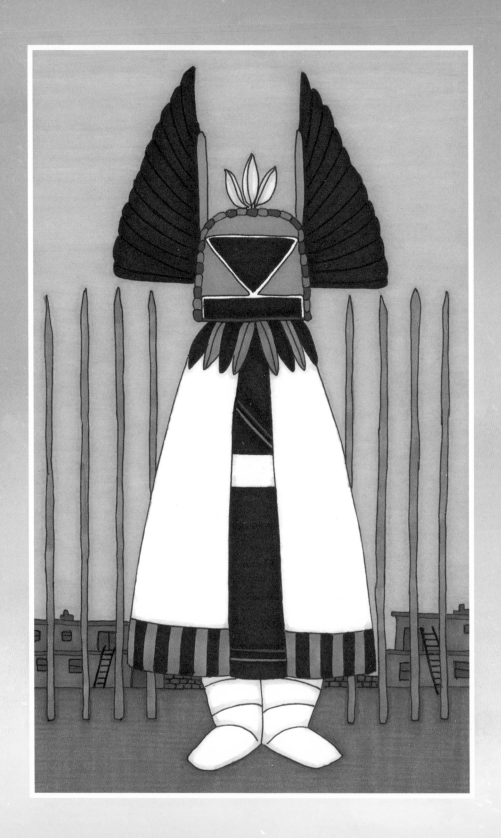

C IS FOR CROW MOTHER
Crow Mother is from Arizona.

She is the mother of all Kachinas, the Hopi people's name for the spirits of nature. Crow Mother wears the dress and boots of a Hopi woman but is masked like a spirit. Kachinas give rainfall, protection, and healing to the people. The people give Kachinas prayer feathers, corn pollen, and respect. This sharing of gifts creates harmony in the world.

Crow Mother teaches the children how to live in peace with the people of the town and how to respect and live in peace with the animals, plants, and spirits of the country.

She comes to the mesas at the first full moon of spring, singing the song of the Kachinas, of how they came to be in this land. Crow Mother comes from the San Francisco Mountains to begin the Powamu ceremony of renewal. She brings with her a basket full of bean sprouts to give a good life to her people for another year.

D IS FOR DURGA

Durga (*DUR-gah*) is from India.

She is the mother goddess of protection. Her name means Beyond Reach, meaning a place like a fort or a sanctuary, a place where nothing bad or scary can come.

This invincible goddess comes riding on her lion, showing she commands great strength. Durga comes when there are too many monsters on the Earth, and they are hurting and scaring her people. She protects her children, and all people are her children. This is a goddess that fights the monsters until they are gone. The monsters she fights are hatred, anger, and injustice. She's there to help when something is mean or unfair. If she ever needs help, other warrior goddesses will come whenever she calls.

In her hands are her many weapons, showing that different weapons are used for different fights. The conch shell is not a weapon but is blown to make the sound of the sacred Om of creation, because Creation is what she fights for.

E IS FOR EPONA

Epona (*ay-PONE-ah*) is from England.

She is the goddess of horses. Her name means Great Mare. The Great Mare is the mother of all horses. Her gift of horses provides milk and meat to her people, the Celts (*Kelts*). The strength of horses lets them travel quickly and carry heavy loads at a time when there are no engines. The Celts are great riders, and they care for their horses very much. A large herd is a blessing from Epona. Because of this, Epona is known as the goddess of plenty, of having lots of good things. She can be seen riding with her mares and foals, carrying a basket of juicy, sweet apples.

Epona is also the Night Mare. She brings special dreams to people. Sometimes the dreams are scary, sometimes they are beautiful, but they are always meaningful. They can let you gallop as fast as a horse, warn you about danger, or show you the way to have a good life.

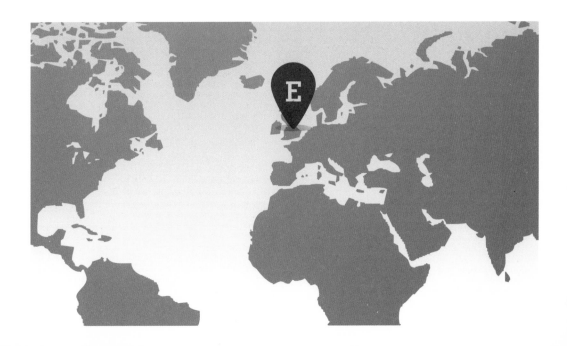

F IS FOR FORTUNA
Fortuna (*for-TOON-ah*) is from Italy.

She is the goddess of fate and fortune. She can bring good luck or bad luck, good fortune or bad fortune. Sometimes what seems to be bad luck can turn out for the good. Sometimes what seems to be good luck is not. She is the goddess of fate because she can see farther than people can. She can see into the future, and she sets a course toward that future, holding her ship's steering wheel.

Fortuna's symbol is the wheel that turns around and around. This can be a spinning wheel for yarn, a game wheel, or a wagon wheel. People may climb her wheel and hope to stay on top, but her wheel will keep going around. Change comes to everyone. Nothing stays the same forever; everything rises and falls to rise again.

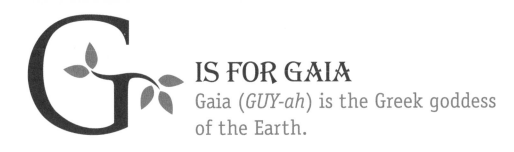

G IS FOR GAIA

Gaia (*GUY-ah*) is the Greek goddess of the Earth.

She can never be separate from the Earth because all of the Earth is her body. She looks up from the ground to the sky she loves. She holds up her hands to bless her children.

Gaia is the mother of all, for everything in nature comes from her, whether animal, tree, or rock. She is the mother of gods and the mother of monsters too. Gaia is always giving birth, and she loves and understands all of her children. She is the power of nature to make new beings and to help those beings grow. She is also the power of nature to recycle what is worn out so it can be something new again.

Gaia provides the place for life to happen. Since she knows all that takes place upon her body, Gaia created the first oracles, the sacred places where the goddesses whisper their secrets to people who would listen.

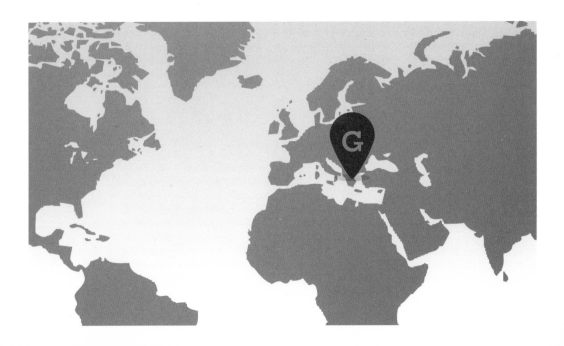

H IS FOR HAYA-AKITSU-HIME

Haya-Akitsu-Hime
(*HI-yah ah-KIT-soo HEE-may*)
is from the islands of Japan.

For the people who follow Shinto (the Way of the Gods), this is the goddess of the surrounding sea. Haya-Akitsu-Hime's ocean is so deep and wide, her salt water so cleansing and healing, that she can swallow all of the evils of the world and dissolve them. She changes those wicked spirits and turns them back into their original beings, taking them back to pure energy.

Haya-Akitsu-Hime teaches her people how to make themselves pure. Sea salt holds her purification and protection magic. People may carry a packet of grains of salt with them to protect them from bad energies throughout the day, or scatter the tiny crystals around a space to clear it.

Before her people come to speak with any of the Kami (the goddesses and gods), they wash their hands and rinse out their mouths with salt water so that they will do and say only what is good and true. When they can, they go to the sea and immerse their bodies in the water to give their pain to Haya-Akitsu-Hime for recycling.

IS FOR ISIS

Isis (*EYE-sis*) is from Egypt.

She is the goddess of magic. She becomes the most powerful of the gods and goddesses by tricking Ra, the sun god, into telling her his secret name, the name that holds his *heka*. Heka is the ancient Egyptian word for magic. It is the power to cast spells to invent new things to create and to destroy.

Isis needs her magic to heal her husband, Osiris, when he is cut into pieces by his jealous brother. Isis gathers him up, spreads her wings over her beloved, speaking her magic words, and brings him back from the land of the dead. His skin is green because he is the god of all the growing things that begin life sleeping within the Earth.

Isis wears on her head the solar disk that represents the fierce Eye of Ra, while on her magician's table is the healing Eye of Horus, who is her child and will be the new sun god. Her great powers are kept in balance by her care for others.

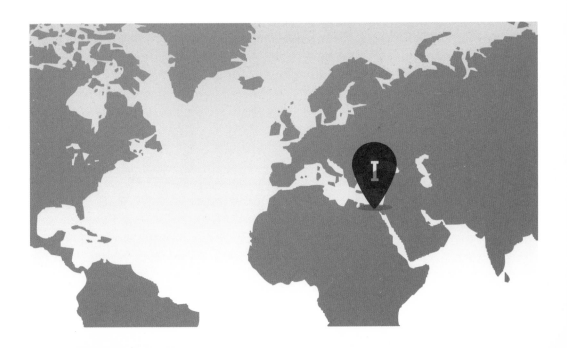

J IS FOR JULUNGGUL

Julunggul *(joo-LOON-gghool)* is from Arnhem Land in Australia.

She is a goddess of creation. Julunggul is an enormous rainbow serpent who sleeps in deep places within the Earth. When she awakens, she travels far and wide across the land, her slithering body leaving wide curving tracks. When the rains come, or when she calls to the frogs to come out of hiding and tickles them until they spill out the water they've been holding in their bellies, these tracks fill up with water and become the rivers and lakes of the world.

Julunggul is a goddess of initiation, of change into another level of life, like a child becoming a grown up. Puberty is a time when people's bodies change. Julunggul makes sure a person's wisdom grows along with their body. She swallows up girls and boys, and inside her body, inside the womb of creation, they learn about their new life, both its pleasures and its responsibilities. When the goddess spits them back out, they have been changed into grown women and men.

K IS FOR KWAN YIN

Kwan Yin is from China.

She is the goddess of compassion, of caring for others. Her name means "She Who Hears the Cries of the World." She sees what people are going through, and she understands and cares. Kwan Yin's compassion is so great that she cares for everyone, for no other reason than that they are beings with feelings. She wants to save all beings from pain.

Kwan Yin can take many forms, with each one showing a part of her compassion. Often she is seen as a woman in flowing robes of pure and shining light. She holds a willow branch in one hand and a blue vase in the other. Blue is the color of wisdom, and the vase holds the nectar of life. She uses the willow branch to sprinkle the holy water on the people who need her healing and ask for her blessing.

This goddess wears a rosary around her neck, with each red bead standing for a living being. When Kwan Yin prays and the bead is turned, the being finds peace and knows the feeling of being at one with the world.

IS FOR THE LADY OF THE LAKE

The Lady of the Lake is from England.

Her name is Nimue, or sometimes Vivian, or sometimes Igraine. The lady of many names is queen of a watery otherworld, a strange but wonderful land that lies beyond the shore. She is the goddess of the lake, the reservoir at the center of an abundant life.

The lakes of England are rich in fresh water, fish, and birds, all the things her people need to live. But the lakes are also tricky and hard to get to know. The shoreline shifts, the mud sucks at your feet, the mists rise, and the way home is lost. The way to the world of magic and spirit is shown instead. The Lady of the Lake may show herself to you, and if she does, she may grant you a wish. Or she could give you a quest, which is a special task to do or journey to take. The swans of her lake are her messengers, bringing to the world her gifts of beauty, love, and magic.

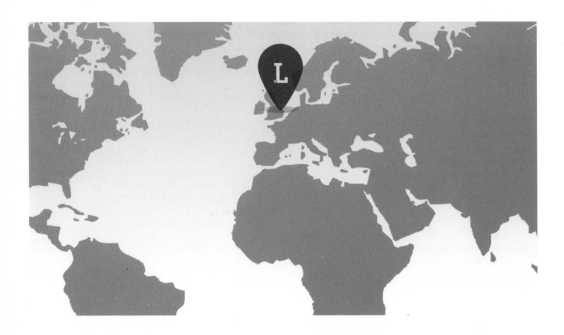

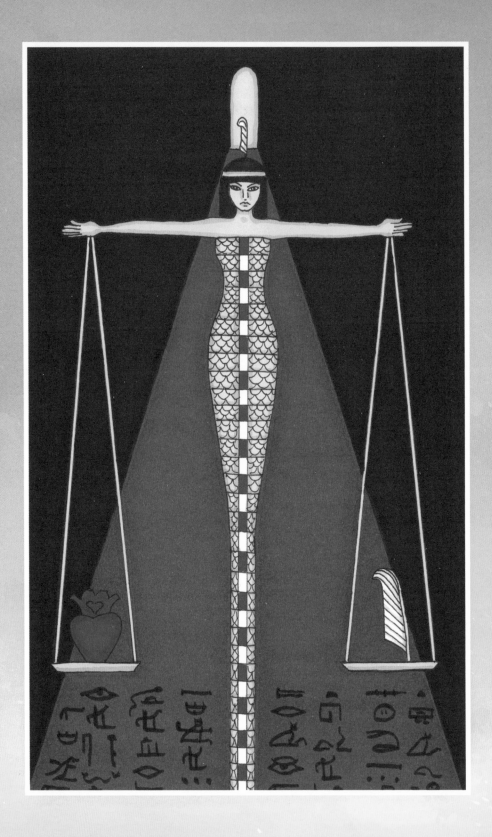

IS FOR MAAT
Maat (*MAAHT*) comes from Egypt.

She is the goddess of truth, balance, law, morality, and justice. The word "Maat" means all of these things together because, in her world, one is cannot be separated from the others. Maat is the foundation of the Universe, the law and balance of the Universe, and her truth. Maat arranges and keeps in order the stars and all the worlds. She does not let the powers of chaos and strife take over all of life. She asks humans to do their part in creating cosmic harmony through behaving well. The universe is a holy place where it is important to stay honest, balanced, and good.

Maat is shown as a woman wearing a feather in her hair. She may have outstretched wings or hold a scepter for power, an ankh for life, or a scale for judgment. Sometimes she becomes the scale itself. She weighs a person's heart and balances it with one of her feathers. For a person with a light heart who is happy and good, she opens the door to a true and beautiful life.

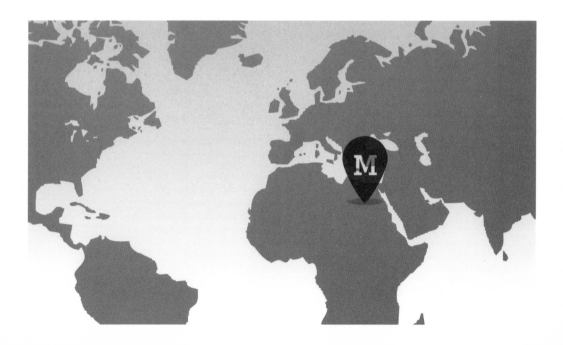

IS FOR THE NORNS

The Norns are from Norway.

The Norns are three sisters who are the goddesses of fate. Their names are Urth (What Has Been), Verthandi (What Is Becoming), and Skuld (What Shall Be).

The Norns can appear to be young or old women, maidens or crones. They live among the roots of the World Tree. It is their job to keep the tree strong and healthy by drawing water from a well to nourish the roots of the tree. As the tree is strong, so are the people, because the tree holds all worlds within it. A wicked dragon lurks below and gnaws at the roots to cause trouble in the worlds, but the Norns will not let the tree die.

The Norns are goddesses of fate because they set limits to what can be done. They create the loom of life, and it is their job to weave its tapestry. The tapestry is not yet complete, for within their frame every person may choose how to act and whether they will help weave the tapestry and feed the living tree through their actions every day.

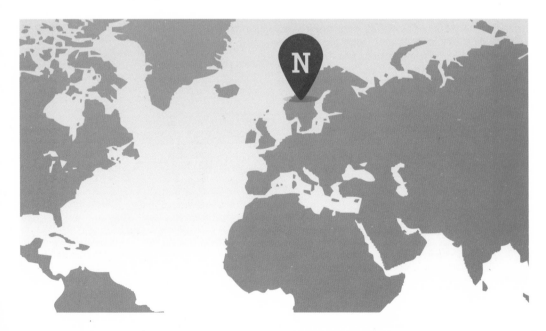

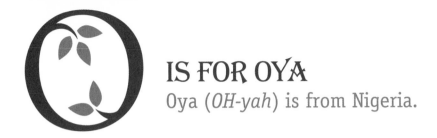

IS FOR OYA

Oya (*OH-yah*) is from Nigeria.

She is the goddess of the whirlwind. She controls the air, rides storms like they are horses, and whirls her beaded horsetail to stir up lightning. Her name means Tearer. That is the power of the whirlwind to rip trees down to their roots. Oya dances over the Earth, twirling in her dress of many colors. She brings change to all she touches and sweeps away the broken things to make room for something new. This goddess changes the world. Her places of power are the places where change happens—like the market, where her people exchange the things they have for the things they want.

Oya wants to change the world because she has known deep sadness and wants to create a world where there is no sadness. Each color of the scarves she ties around her waist is to remember a child who did not have the chance to grow and live. She journeys to the place of creation, to the holy city of Ife (*ee-FEH*). There she dances her prayer for her children's rebirth. She dances up a new world.

P IS FOR PELE
Pele (*PAY-lay*) is from Hawaii.

She is the goddess of the volcano, of fire, and of Earth. It is her fire that creates the volcanoes that rise from the sea, and her volcanoes that create the Hawaiian Islands, which are her home.

Pele can appear as an old woman who can light candles with a snap of her fingers or as a young woman who dances wildly on the rims of craters at the very edge of the volcano. She can also appear in her elements as a river of red running lava, as steam rising from cracked black rock, or as fountains of sparks against the sky.

Hawaii is Pele's home and body. Travelers who pocket stones in Hawaii and take them away may have bad luck until those pieces are returned to her. Every stone and every wonderful thing that is grown on her land belongs to her. They are her gifts to her people. Her people give back by throwing offerings into the crater. They offer sugar cane, hibiscus flowers, sweet berries, evergreen branches, and strands of their own beautiful hair.

IS FOR MAMA QUILLA
Mama Quilla (*KEY-yah*) is from Peru.

Her name means Mother Moon. She is the goddess of the moon, the mother of the sky, and one of the three founders of the Inca nation along with the god of the sun and the god of thunder. When Mama Quilla cries, her tears are made of pure silver.

Her people love her for her beauty and for the blessings her shining face gives them in the dark night. Her people fear for their Mama Quilla during lunar eclipses, when the shadow of the Earth crosses over the face of the Moon. They are afraid an animal is attacking the goddess, and they scare the animal away by shouting and throwing sticks. When her light returns they celebrate, and she beams upon them once more.

Mama Quilla is the goddess of marriage. She protects the mothers and governs the cycles of nature, of women, and of the Moon. She is also the goddess of the calendar, because by studying these natural cycles, she taught her people how to measure the passing of time.

IS FOR RHEA

Rhea (RAY-ah) is from Greece.

Her name means Flow. Her name means Ease. Ease is when you have all you need to feel cozy, safe, and good: food to eat, blankets to snuggle in, and loving kindness from someone close to you. Her name shows how the good things in life, and all the good beings who are born on this Earth, come from her. The milk of life flows from her, easily and beautifully and for all time, to help generation after generation of mothers feed their babies. She is the goddess of motherhood, and she is the mother of the gods.

Rhea wears a turret crown, a crown made from a city wall. The crown and her friendly lions show how strong she is at protecting her people and providing them with safe places to live.

Rhea is married to Chronos, whose name means Time. Time is famous for swallowing up and ending things over and over again. Rhea is famous for saving her baby, the young Zeus, from being swallowed. She saves him so he can grow up to become the god of thunder, who he is meant to be.

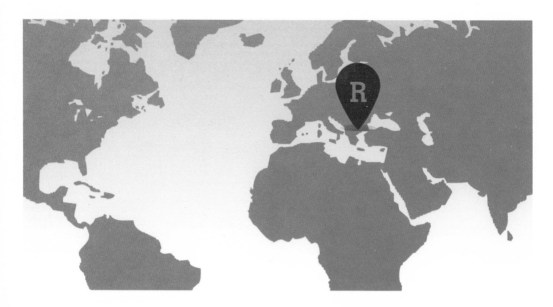

S IS FOR SAMOVILA
Samovila (*sam-oh-VEE-lah*) is from Bulgaria.

She is the goddess of the forest and the guardian of the wild animals who live there. She keeps them safe from careless hunters. She will lead hunters on wrong paths or cause branches to fall on them or stones to turn under their feet. She protects the wild streams that flow in the forest, too, keeping the water pure and clean.

Samovila is a shape-shifter, so she can take on the shape of any animal in the woods. She may be a falcon, a swan, a snake, or a horse. The powerful bear is her special friend. When she appears in human form, she wears a dress made of white feathers.

When she feels playful, Samovila loves to dance. Her circle dances create the magical glades that are found in even the deepest parts of forest. If you are respectful of nature and kind to animals, Samovila may invite you into her circle to dance with her, and heal your body and your heart.

IS FOR TARA

Tara is (*TAH-rah*) from Tibet.

She is the goddess of compassion and wisdom and can be pure spirit, or she might live as a simple shepherd girl. Tara has twenty-one forms, and each has a different color and special power. Green Tara is surrounded by flowers. She is the abundance of the natural world, the comfort of the spiritual world, and the beauty of both.

Green Tara sits on her lotus throne with one leg bent and one outstretched. This position is relaxed but also shows she is ready to spring into action whenever it is needed. At any moment she may leap from her seat to aid someone who is hurting or confused. Besides her legs, the positions of her hands also have meaning. Her right hand is open so that she may give blessings, while her left hand promises protection from harm.

IS FOR USHAS
Ushas *(OO-shahs)* is from India.

Her name means Dawn, and she is the goddess of the first light of morning. When Ushas awakens from sleep, the night is still dark. She rises, and her mother, the sky, dresses her daughter in clothing and jewelry made of hope, light, and life. Her sister, the night, shares her magic with her. The magic of the goddess of the dawn is to see everything and everybody all at once, as if Ushas had a hundred eyes. Nothing is hidden from her sight, and that makes Ushas wise. She sees clearly but does not judge what she sees, and that makes her compassionate.

When Ushas is dressed in light and magic, she is ready to drive her cow-drawn chariot across the sky. She is a playful, happy goddess and is radiant with color, beauty, and joy. She dances ahead of the sun and leads him across the sky, bringing warmth and love to the world along with her lovely light.

V IS FOR VESTA
Vesta (*VEST-ah*) is from Italy.

She is the goddess of the fire of the Earth that is the home fire—the fireplace or the stove or the kitchen, the place that gives warmth and cooked food, the place where the family gathers around. For the city of Rome in Italy, Vesta's round temple held the Earth fire for the city, for the city where many homes of people are gathered together.

Usually Vesta shows herself only in her sacred fire. If she does take human form, she wears a modest, simple dress of plain wool. She does not care for fancy things. She cares about a strong heart, a heart that has courage and endurance. In her hand is the fuel her people use for their fires. When gathered branches are carefully tied together, they make a log that will burn longer and stronger than a pile of sticks will.

Vesta's fire is always burning. Only on March 1, the Roman New Year, is the fire in her temple allowed to go out before being relit. That special lighting renews the strength and heart of the city and all her people.

W IS FOR WHITE BUFFALO CALF WOMAN

White Buffalo Calf Woman comes from South Dakota.

She is a goddess of abundance, healing, and wisdom. White Buffalo Calf Woman comes to her people in their times of need, when their food, the buffalo, is hard to find and the people are hungry.

She comes to show how all beings are connected in the sacred hoop, the holy circle of life. White Buffalo Calf Woman brings the sacred pipe to her people. The smoke rising from the bowl is the breath of Tunkashila, the oldest and wisest being of all. The sacred pipe is held up to each direction around the circle: the east, the south, the west, and the north. Then White Buffalo Calf Woman teaches the words and dances that help the people's prayers be heard by the gods.

When she leaves, the buffalo return. Hope and abundance return with the understanding of how the buffalo and the grass and the people and the spirits all need each other. White Buffalo Calf Woman teaches that when good action is joined by good prayer, all that is needed is given.

IS FOR XOCHIQUETZAL

Xochiquetzal (*show-key-KET-zal*)
is from Mexico.

Her name in the Aztec language means Flower Feather. She is the goddess of flowers and plants, of all that is beautiful, abundant, and wonderful in nature. She wears a crown made of gold, jewels, and the magical green feathers of the quetzal, a bird that means freedom and richness to her people. Every eight years the Aztec people have a huge feast and wear animal and flower masks in honor of the goddess.

Xochiquetzal is the goddess of weaving and other arts, of the beauty that people can make with their hands, like the decorated poncho she wears. She is also the goddess of games, dance, and love—of the fun, sweet, and beautiful things that can happen between people.

Butterflies flutter around Xochiquetzal. Her arms are open; she has flowers in her hands. She invites you to dress up in your fanciest clothes and dance with her and her butterflies.

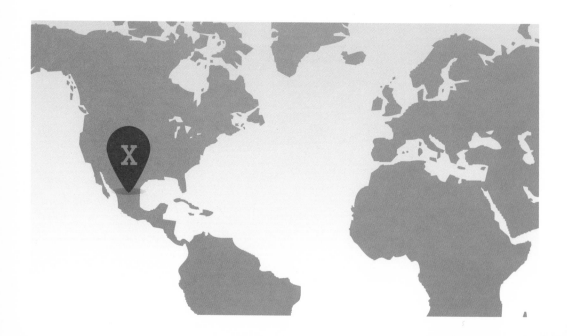

IS FOR YEMAYA
Yemeya *(YEH-mah-yah)* is from Nigeria.

She is the goddess of the ocean, and her name means Mother of the Fishes. Her children are uncountable and fill the seas. Yemaya's part of the ocean is near the top and near the shore—not the deep or dark places of the ocean but the parts where there are plants and fish that people can use for food. She is the creative and giving part of the sea and is called the mother of all, for the ocean gives life to the world.

Yemaya wears blue and white. When she shows herself as a woman, her dress has ruffles that stand for the waves, and seven layers to stand for the seven seas. When Yemaya dances, she sways to the rhythm of the waves, then swirls and twirls faster and faster to show her great power. She is strong and beautiful, and she is mostly kind, but Yemaya will show her fierce side when her children are in danger. She offers the love and protection of a good mother to anyone who feels alone.

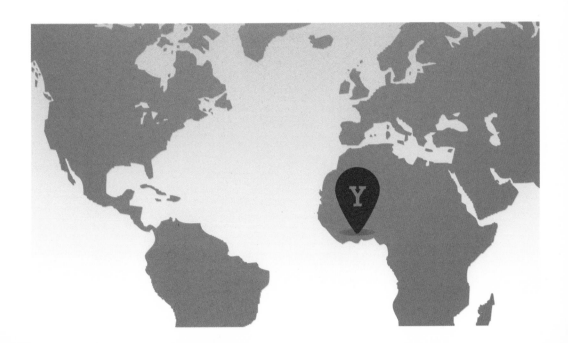

Z IS FOR THE ZORYA
The Zorya (*ZOAR-ee-ah*) come from Russia.

Zorya means Rising Star. The star goddess can appear as one woman or as two sisters or as three. When they are three, they are the Morning Star, the Evening Star, and the Midnight Star. The sisters live on a magical island in a place where the winds of the north, east, and west all meet, and where their father, Dazbog the Sun, has a beautiful palace.

Zorya Utrennyaya (*OO-tren-ee-yah*), the Morning Star, opens the gates of the palace at dawn so that the Sun can ride out on his chariot and begin the day. Her people pray to her every morning for protection and strength for their new day. Zorya Vechernyaya (*veh-CHURN-ee-yah*), the Evening Star, closes the gates of heaven each night when the Sun returns home. Her people pray to her to find their way when they are lost. She is the mother of the stars, who sets them in the sky to be guiding lights for those that live on Earth. The Midnight Star is Zorya Polunochnaya (*poh-LOON-oh-chee-yah*). Every night the Sun sleeps in her arms. She holds and protects him throughout the night until the morning comes and the Sun rises again.

How To Be Friends With Your Goddess

Listen in quietude and stillness
to your wise inner voice, perhaps by gazing into a bowl of still
water like the Pythia of ancient Greece.

Create sacred art like the people of St. John's Church
in Luxembourg, who refresh the paint on their statue of the
Black Madonna every year in thanks for her blessings.

Learn about building and keeping a fire to see spirits
in the flames, like the Ainu people of Japan see Kamui Fuchi
and their ancestors.

Think about new ways to do things that help,
like Skadi of Norway who invented skis so she and her people
could get around in the snow.

About the Author/Artist

ELLEN LORENZI-PRINCE is an artist, writer, and grandmother living in the Pacific Northwest. Ellen has loved goddesses since reading the Greek myths when she was nine years old. She'd found stories where a girl had more choices than death or marriage, as at the end of so many of the classic tales she knew. Finally, she'd found stories of women who had power and used it, moving from adventure to adventure. The myths of the goddesses, their ancient sacred stories, inspired possibilities within her. She hopes this book may inspire the dreams of children today.

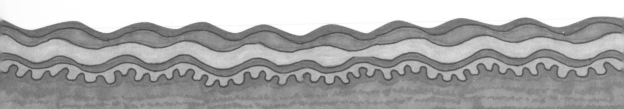